ROCK

SOUNDS OF MUSIC

David and Patricia Armentrout

The Rourke Corporation, Inc.
Vero Beach, Florida 32964

PHOTO CREDITS:
© Bruce Carr: Cover, pages 10, 18; © Al Michaud: title page;
© Robin Schwartz/Intl. Stock: page 4; © Oscar C. Williams: pages 7, 13, 21;
© Reuters/Ron Kuntz/Archive Photos: page 8; © Armentrout: page 12;
© Archive Photos: page 15; © Popperfoto/Archive Photos: page 17

PRODUCED BY:
East Coast Studios, Merritt Island, Florida

EDITORIAL SERVICES:
Susan Albury

Library of Congress Cataloging-in-Publication Data

Armentrout, David. 1962-
    Rock / by David and Patricia Armentrout.
        p. cm. — (Sounds of music)
    Includes bibliographical references (p. 24) and index.
    Summary: A history of rock and roll music from its beginnings in rhythm and blues to the present day, including a discussion of the electric guitar, and rock star Elvis Presley.
    ISBN 0-86593-536-X
    1. Rock music—History and criticism Juvenile literature. [1. Rock music.]
I. Armentrout, Patricia, 1960- II. Title. III. Series
ML3534.A75 1999
781.66'09—dc21   99-14250
                                                                    CIP

Printed in the USA

TABLE OF CONTENTS

LOVE THAT BEAT

Rock-and-roll music became a popular musical style in the 1950s. Its first fans were teenagers looking for a new sound.

Today rock is one of the most popular musical styles in the United States, and in many other countries around the world.

As with most popular music, rock is a combination of musical styles. What makes music "rock"? It's the driving beat and **rhythm** (RITH em).

The Rolling Stones have been a popular rock band for almost four decades.

RHYTHM AND BLUES

Where did rock music come from? The term *rock and roll* was first used by rhythm-and-blues **artists** (ART ests) in the early 1950s. A radio disc jockey named Alan Freed started using the term on the air. The term stuck and was used to describe a new style of rhythm and blues.

In the beginning rock was just a form of rhythm and blues. Then performers added sounds from other musical styles, like country and jazz, which gave rock a sound and feel of its own.

It takes years of practice to become a great guitar player.

THE FIRST ROCKERS

It is impossible to credit one artist with the invention of rock music. Many **musicians** (myu ZISH enz) helped form the new music style.

Little Richard, Chuck Berry, and Bill Haley performed in the 1950s. They all helped pave the way for future rock and rollers. Their music was fast, loud, and had a beat that kids loved to dance to. The **lyrics** (LEER iks), or words, spoke of things young people could relate to.

THE GUITAR

The most famous rock instrument is the guitar. Many rock musicians play electric guitars. Electric guitars can be plugged into an **amplifier** (AM pluh fire) to increase sound.

Guitars have strings made of metal, gut, or nylon. One end of each string is fastened to a tuning screw. The opposite ends are fastened to a bridge on the guitar's soundboard.

You play a guitar by strumming or plucking the strings with your fingers or with a pick.

You tune a guitar by tightening or loosening the tuning screws.

Learning to play an instrument is more fun when you have a good teacher.

If you are going to play drums you may want to buy your parents a set of ear plugs.

SUPERSTARS

A superstar is a performer that becomes wildly popular, and stays popular for many years. One of the biggest rock superstars was Elvis Presley.

During the 1950s Elvis Presley brought the sounds of country together with rhythm and blues. He soon became known for his performance style around the world.

Even now, after his death, Elvis Presley remains a favorite of many. Presley has even been labeled the "king" of rock and roll.

Elvis Presley is known as the "king" of rock and roll.

THE BRITISH INVASION

The 1960s marks a period in American music history called the British Invasion. This is when British rock groups, like the Beatles and the Rolling Stones, began touring in America.

The Beatles already had some hit songs of their own, but they also sang songs written by American artists.

Many parents didn't like the loud, new beat of the Beatles music. Teenagers loved it! Every appearance drew huge crowds. The Beatles soon became the most popular rock group in the world.

The Beatles played for a TV audience on a 1964 Ed Sullivan show.

IT'S MORE THAN MUSIC

Some rock groups rely on more than music to excite their audience. Bands spend millions of dollars on light and sound equipment. Groups combine laser and strobe lights with huge sound systems. Concerts are turned into spectacular light and sound shows.

Some rockers dress in strange or fancy costumes. In the 1970s artists like KISS and Elton John got the audiences' attention by wearing wild-looking clothes.

Expensive light and sound equipment is needed to put on a rock concert.

YOUR FAVORITE STYLE

Do you like the soft sounds of **acoustic guitars** (uh KOO stik guh TARZ) and gentle voices? Then you probably like soft rock. Maybe loud electric guitars and banging drums are more your style. Then you probably like hard rock or heavy metal.

Rock music comes in different forms. Other popular forms of rock are country rock, jazz rock fusion, punk rock, and alternative rock. What is your favorite style?

Playing an instrument well is one of life's greatest pleasures.

LEARNING TO PLAY

Have you ever pictured yourself playing in a band? Anyone can learn to play rock music. Your parents and teachers can help you get started.

Would you like to take saxophone, harmonica, voice, or drum lessons? Maybe you already play the piano, guitar, or trumpet.

If you sing or play an instrument well, you too can make music ROCK 'N ROLL!

GLOSSARY

acoustic guitar (uh KOO stik guh TAR) — a hollowed-body guitar

amplifier (AM pluh fire) — an electronic device used to increase power or sound

artists (ART ests) — people who create and practice an art such as music writers and performers

lyrics (LEER iks) — the words of a song

musician (myu ZISH en) — a writer or performer of music

rhythm (RITH em) — a combination of notes with long and short sounds and rests

INDEX

FURTHER READING

Find out more about music with these helpful books and information sources:

• Ardley, Neil. *Eyewitness Books: Music.* Knopf, 1989
• McLin, Lena. *Pulse: A History of Music.* Kjos West, 1977
• Pascall, Jeremy. *The Illustrated History of Rock Music.* Exeter Books, 1984
• Spence, Keith. *The Young People's Book of Music.* Millbrook Press, 1995
• Wheeler, Tom. *American Guitars: An Illustrated History.* HarperCollins, 1992
• Berlin, Edward A. "Rock Music." Grolier Multimedia Encyclopedia, 1998
• "Guitar." Microsoft Encarta Encyclopedia, 1996
• "Rock Music." Microsoft Encarta Encyclopedia, 1996